LMSW Exam Prep Pocket Study Guide

LMSW Exam Prep Pocket Study Guide

Professional Values, Ethics, and Relationships

Jeremy Schwartz, LCSW

Seeley Street Press

CONTENTS

Published in the United States of America by:
Seeley Street Press, Takoma Park, MD 20912

First Printing, 2023

Paperback ISBN: 978-1960339027
e-Book ISBN: 978-1960339010

Publisher's Cataloging-in-Publication Data:
Names: Schwartz, Jeremy, author.
Title: LMSW Exam Prep Pocket Study Guide: Professional Values, Ethics, and Relationships / Jeremy Schwartz, LCSW
Description: 2023 Edition. | Takoma Park, MD : Seeley Street Press, [2023]
Identifiers: ISBN 978-1960339027
Subjects: LCSH: Social workers – Certification – United States. | Social service – United States – Examinations – Study guides. | Social service – United States – Examinations, questions, etc.
Classification: LOC: HV40.52.A74 2023 | DDC: 361.3076—dc23

FROM THE AUTHOR

Thank you for making the *LMSW Exam Prep Pocket Study Guides* a part of your study plan as you work toward getting licensed. If you are like most readers picking up this book, chances are you already have significant knowledge and skills in social work. You have spent the past two to three years, at least, in an accredited Master of Social Work program. You may have an undergraduate degree in social work or a related field as well. Now, having reached the termination phase of your MSW studies, you are preparing to pursue licensure or certification in your U.S. state or Canadian province as a professional social worker.

All 50 U.S. states, as well as the District of Columbia, the U.S. Virgin Islands, Guam, the Northern Mariana Islands, and all 10 Canadian provinces are members of the Association of Social Work Boards (ASWB®), the organization that owns and maintains the social work licensing exams. Each state or province has its own licensing terms and requirements. Earning a passing score on this exam is a key milestone in your professional journey as a social worker.

Your passing score on this exam will get you to the next step in your career. Reach out to me at jeremy.d.schwartz@gmail.com if I can be of help. I am available for private tutoring, and would love to hear about your experiences working with this book.

Wishing you success on this journey,

Jeremy

Exam Overview

The ASWB Master's Level exam requires you to know about many different social work topics, even if you plan to specialize in a specific field of practice. As you engage in your content review, think about developing an understanding that is very broad, even if not so deep in every area. You do not need to be an expert in everything! Having a general knowledge about many topic areas is key to your success.

There are 4 content areas covered on the ASWB Master's Level exam:

Human Development and Behavior

Assessment and Intervention Planning

Intervention Methods and Theories

Professional Values, Ethics, and Relationships

This pocket study guide will prepare you specifically for the Professional Values, Ethics, and Relationships exam questions, while also empowering you to be a strong test taker and improve your skills for the entire exam, so that you can earn your passing score and get licensed.

Content Review: Professional Values, Ethics, and Relationships

Social Work Codes of Ethics

The exam requires that you are familiar with, and that you are able to apply, professional social work ethics standards in your work with clients. Social workers in the United States should be familiar with the *National Association of Social Workers (NASW) Code of Ethics*, and social workers in Canada should be familiar with the *Canadian Association of Social Workers (CASW) Code of Ethics*. State and provincial boards of social work have adopted these codes as the basis by which they evaluate professional conduct. Either one will prepare you for this exam content area.

All social workers are held to ethical standards regardless of membership in NASW, CASW, or any other organization. Licensing boards use these ethical principles in the adjudication of disciplinary matters. Codes of ethics may also be utilized in legal disputes as they are a standard, widely accepted reference for understanding social workers' professional duties as well as standards of care.

Social Work Core Values

Perhaps you decided to become a social worker when you realized that the values of the profession matched your own. As a profession grounded in humanistic and altruistic philosophies, social work maintains as its core values the following: service, social justice, human dignity, the importance of human relationships, integrity, and competence.

These core values are included in both the

NASW Code of Ethics and the *CASW Code of Ethics*:

Service

Social work is about using your skills to help people. As an ethical principle, the primary goal for social workers is to help those in need and respond to social problems.

Social Justice

A social justice framework seeks to reduce inequalities such as discrimination and oppression and to address the systems that privilege some groups of people over others. Social workers support policies that provide equal economic opportunities for all people.

Human Dignity

Social workers support diversity and advocate for marginalized and oppressed groups. The value of human dignity also supports a social worker's non-judgmental stance and use of unconditional positive regard in client-centered relationships.

Importance of Human Relationships

One of the most important aspects of social work practice is the helping relationship. Social workers also recognize the importance of human relationships more broadly, and use relationships as a vehicle for social change. In strengthening relationships among people, social workers promote and enhance well being at all levels.

Integrity

Social workers must act honestly and behave in a trustworthy manner. Social workers should practice self-care in order to support their ability to practice ethically and responsibly.

Competence

Competence as a social work value goes beyond the ability to carry out specific interventions.

Social workers must utilize cognitive, critical, and self-reflective abilities to perform in interpersonal, professional relationships. Further, social workers should only practice within their areas of competence, referring to other professionals when needed.

Key Concepts in Social Work Ethics

Responsibility to Clients

According to the *NASW Code of Ethics*, social workers' primary responsibility is to promote client well-being. Clients' interests are, in general, the primary focus. The *Code of Ethics* further states that social workers are not to take unfair advantage of a professional relationship nor to exploit others for their own interests. Social workers should not prioritize their own self-interest over the interests of the client.

Supporting Client Self-Determination

An important social work value is supporting

the rights of clients to make their own choices in their lives. Except in cases of imminent danger to self or others, social workers should not make choices on behalf of clients that go against their wishes, nor attempt to influence client decision-making.

Confidentiality and Its Limits

In general, information that clients share with social workers is confidential. Social workers should take measures to ensure client privacy. However, social workers are required to break client confidentiality in certain circumstances related to client danger to self or others, child abuse or neglect, and elder abuse. Social workers should explain to clients their policies related to confidentiality and its limits.

Duty to Warn and Protect

The concept of "duty to warn and protect" refers to a mental health professional's obligation to inform potential victims, as well as the appropriate authorities, when a client threatens to physically harm others. In the United States, the concept of duty to warn comes from case law, specifically *Tarasoff v. Regents of the University of California*. Similarly, in Canada, courts have found that the duty to warn others of imminent danger can outweigh professionals' responsibility to maintain client confidentiality.

Informed Consent

Informed consent is the process by which a client grants a social worker and/or agency permission to use specific interventions. Informed consent should be based on a full disclosure of all information the client will need in order to make this decision. An informed consent document should include the purpose of the proposed treatment, risks of the proposed treatment, and any alternatives to the proposed treatment. This allows clients to decide for themselves whether or not they would like to proceed.

In most cases, informed consent is necessary before providing social work services. When working with children, the social worker should obtain informed consent from the parent or guardian and verbal **assent** from the child.

Working with Mandated Clients

When working with court-mandated and other involuntary clients, social workers should pay attention to potential challenges in engagement as well as their dual roles and responsibilities in relation to the client and the court. With court mandated treatment there are particular limits to confidentiality as the social worker must report compliance or noncompliance, and possibly more detailed assessment and treatment information, to the court. Social workers should discuss these issues openly with clients and validate clients' experiences related to the involuntary nature of services.

Professional Boundaries

Social workers should maintain appropriate professional boundaries in order to avoid harming clients and in order to avoid harming the public's trust in the social work profession.

Avoiding Dual Relationships

Dual relationships are defined as situations in which a social worker and client experience multiple roles in relation to one another. Dual relationships create the potential for ethical violations and harm to clients. At the same time, dual relationships may at times be unavoidable. Dual or multiple relationships may involve professional, social, and/or business roles. Dual relationships can create the potential for boundary crossing, and can pose ethical concerns. Because of this, dual or multiple relationships are at times unethical.

According to the *NASW Code of Ethics*, social workers should not engage in dual or multiple relationships with current or former clients when they pose a risk of exploitation or harm. At the same time, dual or multiple relationships are at times unavoidable, and must be navigated with clear, appropriate, and culturally sensitive boundaries.

Social workers may encounter conflicts, or

potential conflicts, between their professional roles and relationships and their social, religious, sexual, or business roles or relationships. These conflicts are not always unethical, but they do carry the potential for problematic or unethical boundary crossings and boundary violations. A social worker might join a neighborhood association or community board and find that a client is also involved. Or, a social worker who attends religious services may see clients in that setting on a regular basis. These situations should be handled with care to prevent boundary violations or breaches of confidentiality.

Managing Boundary Crossings and Avoiding Boundary Violations

Boundary crossings are not inherently unethical, but they do pose the potential for harm. A boundary crossing involves bending, but not necessarily breaking, professional boundaries with a client.

One example of a boundary crossing would be

attending a client's wedding or graduation. While the social worker has no obligation to attend, and can decline based on their own personal limits, attendance at a client's significant life event is generally permissible and ethical if handled with sensitive and appropriate boundaries. If a social worker does attend a client's life event, it should be at the request of the client and the therapist must be careful to maintain confidentiality of the social worker - client relationship. The social worker, of course, should consider the clinical implications of attending or not attending the event.

Boundary violations are exploitative, manipulative, deceptive, or coercive actions that are harmful to a client.

Social workers should never engage in sexual contact with current clients. According to the *NASW Code of Ethics*, social workers should also not engage in sexual relationships with client's relatives if this would create a risk of exploitation or harm to the client. (This would nearly always be the case, and so you should not do it!)

Similarly, social workers are not permitted to engage in sexual relationships with former clients, unless the social worker assumes the burden of demonstrating that the client was not intentionally or unintentionally coerced, exploited, or manipulated. Again, this would be difficult to demonstrate, so it is definitely best to avoid entering into this situation.

In addition, social workers should not provide services to a former sexual or romantic partner.

Self-Disclosure

An important aspect of the helping relationship is the social worker's professional use of self. However, the social worker's disclosure of information about themself and their life is a delicate issue that must be handled in a thoughtful manner. Self-disclosure should be used only for the benefit of the client, and careful attention must be paid to boundaries and to the clinical implications of the disclosure.

Social Media and Online Searches

Social workers' use of social media websites and applications creates the potential for boundary crossings. According to the *NASW Code of Ethics,* social workers should be aware of their personal affiliations and online presence and of how their involvement online may impact their ability to work effectively with particular clients.

According to the *NASW Code of Ethics*, social workers should not accept connection requests from clients on social networking sites, and should not engage in personal relationships with clients on social media. This is to prevent boundary confusion, dual relationships, and potential harm. Social workers should also be aware of information they post online, including on social media, and its potential impact on their ability to work with particular clients and client groups. However, social workers may use social media in professional ways without engaging in direct communication with clients.

In general, social workers should not conduct

online searches about clients without their consent. Exceptions to this are in cases of imminent danger.

Ethical Dilemmas

An **ethical dilemma** involves a difficult choice between two or more courses of action. This choice presents itself when the social worker encounters a situation in which multiple ethical principles appear to require conflicting professional actions. Ethical problem solving begins with identifying the ethical principles at stake, and then requires determining whether or not there is in fact an ethical dilemma, weighing ethical issues in light of social work values and principles, proposing a course of action in line with social work values and principles, and implementing that course of action.

Termination and Social Work Ethics

In an ideal scenario, clients would complete the intervention phase of treatment, and a review of progress in the evaluation phase would demonstrate that goals have been met. Following this, clients would work through the **termination phase** before ending the social worker - client relationship.

While this can and does happen, there are many other scenarios in which termination is more complex. Termination may occur because a client requires a different level of treatment, or due to reasons related to insurance or payment. Or, clients may choose to terminate even if goals have not been met.

When the social worker, rather than the client, initiates termination, there are many ethical issues to consider in order to avoid client abandonment. Social workers must assess for safety, only terminating if the client does not pose a danger to self or others. If a client is being referred to a different provider while there are safety concerns, the social worker should ensure that the client has initiated treatment with the new provider before terminating treatment with that client.

In cases of **termination due to non-payment**, there are specific ethical considerations. Social workers must first ensure that clients have been informed of their outstanding balance. This may take the form of a written invoice. The social worker must also discuss the implications of non-payment so that the client is aware that services will be terminated if they do not make payment. As mentioned, the social worker must also assess for safety, only terminating services if the client does not pose a danger to self or others.

A social worker should not terminate services in order to pursue a business relationship with a client. In addition, a social worker should not terminate services in order to pursue a social or sexual relationship with a client.

Follow-Up After Termination

In some cases, it is appropriate and helpful to **follow up** with clients following the termination of services. Depending on client need, it may be necessary to follow up with a client to ensure that they have connected with the ongoing care to which they were referred. It is also helpful in some cases to reach out to a former client in order to reassess the need for further services.

Supervision

The *NASW Code of Ethics* states that social workers should provide supervision only within their areas of knowledge and competence. In addition, social work supervisors must set clear, appropriate, and culturally sensitive boundaries. Social workers providing supervision or consultation should not engage in dual or multiple relationships that pose potential harm to the supervisee.

Supervisors and supervisees should be attentive to issues of parallel process. **Parallel process** describes the ways in which the social worker's relationship with their supervisor impacts the social worker's relationship with clients.

Transference and Countertransference

Social workers should use supervision to discuss

issues of transference and countertransference. **Transference** refers to a client's feelings, based on other past or present relationships, that are transferred to the client's relationship with the social worker. **Countertransference** refers to a social worker or therapist's feelings, based on other past or present relationships, that are transferred to the social worker's relationship with a client.

Client Reluctance and Resistance

It is normal to encounter client reluctance as well as client resistance. The social worker should use understanding and empathy, as well as negotiation skills when appropriate, in order to engage clients and work through resistance. When facing client resistance, the use of supervision can also be helpful.

Language Interpretation

Social workers should use qualified **language interpreters**, rather than client's family members or agency staff not trained in interpretation, when they do not speak or sign the client's requested language. The social worker should face the client, rather than the interpreter, and should speak and listen directly to the client.

Representing Oneself to Clients and to the Public

According to the *NASW Code of Ethics*, social workers should accurately represent their education and credentials to clients, agencies, and the public.

Working with Multidisciplinary Teams

When working with multidisciplinary teams, social workers have the opportunity to provide a psychosocial perspective to the team's work in helping mutual clients. Social workers should use teamwork skills to collaborate effectively with other professionals, considering team interactions as an aspect of mezzo-level social work practice.

Student Interns

It is important for student interns to inform clients of their student intern status. Student interns should inform clients of when their field practicum will end, in order to prepare clients for termination, and should also inform clients of their supervision arrangement so that clients are aware of what information will be shared and with whom.

Impairment of Colleagues

According to the *NASW Code of Ethics*, social workers who become aware that a colleague is impaired due to substance abuse, mental health problems, or other personal problems should speak directly with that colleague when feasible in order to assist the colleague in addressing the issue. Only once this has been done, and if the colleague has not taken steps to address this impairment, should a social worker take action through other channels.

Continuing Education

Learning in social work, as in any field, is a life-long endeavor. After completing their graduate education, social workers should pursue continuing education and training throughout their career. Many licensing boards will require continuing education hours, but social workers should seek out training opportunities and also review professional literature on a regular basis even if there is not a specific hour or credit requirement.

Preventing, Recognizing, and Managing Burnout

While it is best to prevent burnout altogether, it is also necessary to have skills for recognizing and managing burnout when it arises.

Best practices for addressing burnout include practicing self-care, engaging in mindfulness activities, and connecting with other professionals. In cases of burnout, a multi-faceted approach is often needed. **Burnout** takes the forms of depletion or exhaustion, increased distancing mentally from one's professional role, negativity or cynicism toward one's work, and reduced effectiveness in a professional role. Addressing burnout requires both structural and individual changes. At the individual level, addressing burnout requires multiple, ongoing forms of self-care (i.e., a lifestyle rather than a vacation), along with engagement with a community of colleagues.

Self-Care

It is well-established that social workers should prioritize self-care, but this is also easier said than done. **Self-care** is more than occasionally treating yourself to something nice or taking a break, but instead requires structural measures to manage the structural problems that can potentially lead to burnout. Best practices for self-care include plenty of rest, healthy boundaries, and utilizing social support. It is important to have a self-care plan and follow it consistently.

Compassion Fatigue

Compassion fatigue includes both emotional

and physical exhaustion that inhibit one's capacity to empathize and feel compassion for others. It is caused by exposure to traumatic material and may have a sudden, rapid onset. Its symptoms can mirror those of post traumatic stress disorder.

Social Worker Safety

Attending to **worker safety** is important for any agency. Best practices for attending to worker safety include conducting a thorough clinical risk assessment for each client, providing high quality safety training for workers, and convening an agency safety committee in order to oversee the implementation of safe workplace strategies.

Subpoenas

Receipt of a subpoena from an attorney is not an ethical reason to disclose client information without consent. A subpoena is not the same as a court order, and an attorney who is not a judge does not have the authority to compel the release of records. In response to a subpoena, a social worker should claim privilege and should not provide records unless a court order is issued.

Court Orders

A court order signed by a judge does compel the release of confidential information. Even so, the social worker should protect the client by attempting to limit the scope of records required, and should request that records remain under seal.

Mandated Reporting

Suspected Child Abuse or Neglect

Social workers are **mandated reporters** of **suspected child abuse or neglect**, and should file such reports with the state or local jurisdiction based on jurisdictional requirements. As a mandated reporter, the social worker is responsible for making a report anytime there is suspected abuse or neglect of a child. This does not require the social worker to investigate further, although that may in some cases also be appropriate depending on the setting and situational factors. While consulting with a supervisor may also at times be appropriate or necessary for the social worker's assessment or intervention process, making the report of suspected child abuse or neglect comes first and is not contingent on any supervisory guidance.

Suspected Elder Abuse or Neglect

In many states, social workers are also legally mandated to report situations of suspected elder abuse. Social workers should be aware of **elder abuse**, its signs, and reporting requirements. Elder abuse can include physical abuse, emotional or psychological abuse, financial exploitation, and neglect. Elder abuse reporting goes through state and local adult protective services (APS) agencies, which investigate and assess cases of suspected mistreatment of older adults as well as other vulnerable adults including abuse, neglect, and financial exploitation.

Whenever possible, clients should be informed about reports being made by a social worker.

Practice Questions

Exam Question Format

Before 2023, ASWB exam questions all had 4 answer choices each (A, B, C, and D). Starting in January 2023, some test questions will have 3 answer choices (A, B, and C) while other questions will have 4 answer choices (A, B, C, and D). The practice questions in this book are updated for this 2023 format.

The ASWB has shared that they will continue to phase in more three-option questions in the coming months, with a goal of transitioning completely to a three-option format by 2025.

So, if you hear rumors about how the exam is changing this year, this is it! There are no other significant changes to the test format that have been announced for this year, and nothing you need to do differently in order to prepare. Just know that some questions will only have 3 answer choices, so that this does not cause any surprise or confusion on your exam day.

As always, it is important to answer every question and to not leave any questions blank. While most multiple choice exams give you a 25% chance of guessing correctly even if you do not know the answer, this update to the exam gives you even more of a benefit for guessing. On questions with 3 answer choices, you have a 33% chance of guessing correctly even if you have no idea which answer is correct.

Of course, you should incorporate the other test-taking techniques in this guide as well, along with a thorough review of the content. Still, let this change be to your benefit as you work toward earning your passing score.

Test Center Policies

Another change to the testing process in 2023 is that exam candidates will be permitted to retrieve snacks from the test center lockers and eat in the waiting area during the examination. While the time still counts, this allows you to refuel during a break before going back to check over your answers.

Lastly, the policy on electronic devices has changed. While you will need to store your cell phone in your locker for the duration of the exam, you will no longer be required to seal it in the special bag that was used previously.

Practice Questions

Below you will find 60 practice questions so that you can test your knowledge of the professional values, ethics, and relationships content for the ASWB Master's level exam. When you are ready, take out a pen and paper to record your answers. Following this set of practice questions, there will be an answer key so you can check your work, followed by detailed answer explanations.

1. Which of the following is NOT an ethical reason to disclose client information without consent?

A. The social worker receives a subpoena from an attorney
B. The social worker receives a court order signed by a judge
C. The client is at imminent risk of suicide
D. The social worker suspects child abuse or neglect

2. A child meets with a school social worker, who notices a cast on his arm. The child states that he had to go to the hospital after his father threw him down the stairs, but that it was his fault because he misbehaved. He states he will make sure it does not happen again and that there is nothing to worry about. What should the social worker do FIRST?

A. Ask a supervisor if the incident should be reported
B. Report the incident to the state or local child protection agency
C. Schedule an appointment with the parents to find out more about what happened
D. Check with the hospital where the child received the cast to find out how severe the injury was

3. A social worker is working with a client who was recently diagnosed with a terminal illness. The social worker asks the client if he has a will, and encourages the client to include the therapist in his

will since the social worker has played a significant role in his life. This action by the social worker is:

A. Ethical, because the social worker is an important person in the client's life
B. Unethical, because the social worker is prioritizing their own self-interest over the client's best interest
C. Ethical, because the client still has the choice of whether or not to take this action

4. Social justice is BEST defined as:

A. The belief that every person deserves equal rights and opportunities
B. The idea that everyone should have equal economic resources
C. A principle that guides macro social work practice

5. A social worker receives a connection request from a former client on a professional networking site. The client recently started a new business, which had been a significant goal of his during his

sessions with the social worker. The social worker should:

A. Accept the connection request to honor the former client's progress
B. Decline the connection request
C. Ask a supervisor how to handle the situation
D. Respond to the connection request with open-ended questions in order to ascertain the former client's intentions

6. After terminating treatment, a client requests a copy of his records and completes a signed authorization for the records to be mailed to him. The social worker reviews the chart and confirms that there is no information in the records that is likely to be harmful to the client. The social worker should NEXT:

A. Inform the client that records requests must be completed in person so that the social worker can assist the client in interpreting the information they contain.
B. Send the records to the client, and offer to

meet with the client if he would like assistance in interpreting them.

C. Inform the client that a valid reason for the request must be provided before the social worker can proceed

D. Invoke client-therapist privilege and ask a judge to invalidate the request for records.

7. A social worker is working with a client who begins to exhibit symptoms consistent with a diagnosis of schizophrenia. The social worker has no training in how to help clients with schizophrenia. What should the social worker do NEXT?

A. Read about evidence-based interventions for schizophrenia

B. Refer the client to a support group

C. Refer the client to a colleague with experience working with clients who have psychotic disorders

8. All of the following are true statements about cultural competence EXCEPT:

A. The *NASW Code of Ethics* includes standards on cultural competence and diversity
B. Cultural competence requires a flexible and individualized approach
C. Social workers should support policies that respect difference and human rights
D. Social workers should only treat clients with the same cultural background as their own.

9. Which of the following is true regarding supervision in social work practice?

A. Supervision should focus primarily on administrative tasks.
B. Supervision is unnecessary except for student interns.
C. Supervision can assist the social worker in addressing issues of countertransference.
D. Supervision should be provided only by licensed clinical social workers.

10. Which of the following is a true statement about social workers' ethical responsibilities with regard to social justice issues?

A. Social workers must remain neutral on controversial issues.

B. Social workers have a responsibility to engage in social and political action.

C. Social workers should focus exclusively on clinical practice.

D. Social workers should engage primarily in macro practice.

11. All of the following are true regarding dual relationships EXCEPT:

A. Dual relationships can create the potential for boundary crossings

B. Dual relationships should always be avoided

C. Dual relationships can pose ethical concerns

D. Dual relationships are at times unethical

12. According to the professional value of competence, social workers should:

A. Report any colleagues who appear to be incompetent

B. Engage in regular competency testing

C. Practice in areas for which they are qualified, and strive to increase their knowledge

D. Not begin working with clients until they have completed their professional education

13. A client invites a social worker to attend the client's high school graduation ceremony. The social worker should NEXT:

A. Explore the clinical implications of the social worker's attendance or non-attendance

B. Request a consultation with an ethics expert

C. Inform the client that this is not something that social workers do

14. According to the *NASW Code of Ethics*, all of the following are core values of the social work profession EXCEPT:

A. Service

B. Exploration

C. Integrity

D. Social justice

15. Which of the following should be included in an informed consent document?

A. Purpose of the proposed treatment
B. Risks of the proposed treatment
C. Alternatives to the proposed treatment
D. All of the above

16. A social work colleague confides in you that she drank two beers in the morning before coming to work. According to the *NASW Code of Ethics*, you should FIRST:

A. Report the incident to your state licensing board
B. Discuss the situation with your supervisor
C. Call 911 so she can be taken to the emergency room for a psychiatric evaluation
D. Discuss your concerns with the colleague and assist her in making a plan to address her drinking

17. After working during a period of numerous client crises and difficult interpersonal dynamics in

his agency, a social worker begins to notice symptoms of burnout. To best address the symptoms of burnout, the social worker should:

A. Prioritize self-care
B. Engage in mindfulness activities
C. Connect with other professionals
D. All of the above

18. In conducting research on young children, the researcher should:

A. Obtain informed consent of the parent or guardian and verbal assent from the child participants
B. Obtain informed consent of both the parent or guardian and the child
C. Obtain assent of both the parent or guardian and the child
D. Obtain verbal assent from the parent or guardian and informed consent from the child

19. The concept of "duty to warn" refers to:

A. A social worker's status as a mandated reporter for cases of suspected child abuse or neglect
B. A responsibility to inform potential victims, as well as authorities, when a client threatens to inflict physical harm on others
C. A component of the institutional review board process for approving research on human subjects

20. Professional development consists of all of the following EXCEPT:

A. Reviewing published literature
B. Attending in-service trainings
C. Participating in workshops related to social work practice
D. Conducting intake assessments

21. When providing services to clients, social work student interns should do all of the following EXCEPT:

A. Inform clients that services are being provided by a student
B. Discuss the student's end date and the process for termination
C. Identify as social workers when introducing themselves to clients
D. Inform clients of the student's supervision arrangement and what information will be shared with supervisors

22. In order to maintain the confidentiality of client information, social workers should do which of the following:

A. When information must be disclosed, disclose only the minimum amount of confidential information necessary to achieve the purpose of the disclosure
B. Avoid discussing confidential information in public or semipublic areas

C. Ensure that clients' records are stored in a secure location

D. All of the above

23. Which of the following is NOT true regarding time management?

A. Time management aims to increase effectiveness and productivity.

B. Time management is used in both business and personal applications.

C. Time management is best implemented by addressing only urgent issues and devoting most time to "putting out fires."

D. Time management involves categorizing activities based on importance and urgency.

24. Upon hiring a new employee, a social work administrator should FIRST:

A. Explore likely countertransferential issues

B. Review the job description with the employee and provide them with a copy of it

C. Conduct a comprehensive biopsychosocial assessment

D. Develop a social relationship with the employee

25. Compassion fatigue is BEST defined as:

A. Being tired after a long day at the office as a compassionate social worker

B. Emotional and physical exhaustion that inhibits one's capacity to empathize or feel compassion for others

C. An ego defense mechanism

26. A social worker recently began working in an administrative role, which requires that they supervise staff and develop a system for evaluating employee performance. In this role, the social worker should NOT:

A. Engage in dual relationships with supervisees

B. Set culturally sensitive boundaries

C. Supervise only within their areas of knowledge and competence

27. A client meets with a social worker for the first time. At the beginning of the session, the client informs the social worker that the client uses they/them pronouns. To best support the client's dignity and right to self-determination, the social worker should:

A. Conduct a focused biopsychosocial assessment with an emphasis on the client's gender identity
B. Thank the client for sharing their pronouns and use they/them pronouns when referring to the client
C. Ask the client how long they have used these pronouns
D. Ignore this information as it is not the focus of the session

28. A hospital social worker observes that a colleague has been acting differently in recent weeks. The colleague has been drinking heavily at after-work happy hours and has been arriving late to morning staff meetings. The colleague has been away from her desk for long periods of time,

and has not kept up with documentation require-ments. To address this issue, the social worker should FIRST:

A. Report the colleague's impairment to the attending physician
B. Discuss the issue with the social work de-partment supervisor
C. Inform the relevant professional licensing board
D. Discuss these concerns with the colleague directly

29. All of the following are signs of burnout EXCEPT:

A. Physical exhaustion
B. Feeling ineffective in one's work
C. Increased irritability
D. Scheduling of vacation and personal time

30. Which of the following is true regarding confidentiality when conducting couples therapy?

A. Couples therapy poses no specific challenges regarding confidentiality, and so confidentiality issues should be handled the same as in individual therapy
B. Social workers should seek agreement among the parties involved regarding the confidentiality of information shared
C. Information shared in couples counseling is not confidential

31. Which of the following is a true statement regarding burnout?

A. Burnout is clear evidence that a social worker has not prioritized self-care.
B. It is very common to experience burnout in social work.
C. Burnout is always the fault of the individual.
D. Resilient social workers do not experience burnout.

32. All of the following are reasons to terminate services to a client EXCEPT:

A. The client has an unpaid balance, the consequences of non-payment have been discussed with the client, and the client does not pose a danger to self or others
B. The client has reached their goals and does not require further services
C. The client's insurance coverage has changed and the client is being referred to a practice that accepts the new insurance
D. The client and social worker wish to pursue a business venture while avoiding dual or multiple relationships

33. A social worker receives a subpoena from an attorney requesting treatment records for a former client. The social worker should:

A. File a motion to quash the subpoena
B. Release the records requested
C. Ignore the subpoena
D. Redact information from the records

34. Based on the *Tarasoff* decision:

A. Mental health professionals have a duty to warn and protect individuals who are threatened with physical harm by a client.
B. Client information is entirely confidential and can never be released without client consent.
C. Social workers should break confidentiality when a client is at risk of suicide.
D. Clients can be admitted to a hospital involuntarily when they pose a danger to themselves or others.

35. Which of the following is TRUE regarding social workers' presence on social media websites and applications?

A. Social workers should never utilize social media
B. Social media use creates the potential for boundary crossings
C. Social media use is prohibited by the professional *Code of Ethics*

D. Social workers should use social media for personal, non-professional purposes only

36. Confidentiality of client information must be preserved:

A. For the duration of the social worker - client relationship
B. For 5 years following termination
C. For 3 years following termination
D. Indefinitely, even after a client is deceased

37. A social worker has an account on a mobile dating application and receives a message from a former client. The former client asks the social worker if she would like to meet for coffee. The social worker should NEXT:

A. Consult an ethics expert to find out how to best handle the situation
B. Inform the former client that the social worker is actually no longer single
C. Meet for coffee with the former client
D. Decline the former client's invitation

38. An ethical dilemma refers to:

A. A situation in which a social worker is unknowingly acting in an unethical manner
B. A situation in which following one ethical principle appears to require going against a different ethical principle
C. A situation in which a social worker is knowingly acting in an unethical manner
D. A legal determination of unethical behavior

39. Which of the following is true regarding professional codes of ethics?

A. They provide a list of all ethical dilemmas a social worker may encounter
B. They provide step-by-step instructions for how to handle each ethical dilemma
C. They include core values and ethical principles
D. They contain recommendations but not requirements

40. To address the impacts of structural racism, social workers should:

A. Engage in social and political action
B. Attend cultural competency trainings
C. Discuss countertransference in supervision
D. Maintain neutrality and objectivity

41. All of the following are true regarding social work ethics EXCEPT:

A. Social workers are prohibited from having sexual relationships with current clients
B. Dual relationships should be avoided when possible
C. Client self-determination is always the social worker's main priority

42. A client discloses that he is feeling attracted toward his social worker. The social worker should:

A. Terminate services immediately
B. Refer the client to a social worker of a different gender

C. Tell the client that these feelings are inappropriate

D. Explore the client's feelings while maintaining appropriate boundaries

43. A White social worker employed by a Native American tribal health center finds that he is often offending clients as he does not understand cultural norms in the community in which he is working. What should the social worker do NEXT?

A. Request an ethics consultation

B. Seek cultural competency training and education relevant to the population he is working with

C. Ask clients to educate him about Native American culture so he can better understand cultural norms and values

D. Attend a Native American cultural event to immerse himself in the community

44. Which of the following is a true statement regarding the relationship between social policy and social work practice?

A. Social work practitioners should remain neutral on issues of social policy.
B. Social policy determines, to a significant extent, the way that social work is practiced.
C. Social policy and social work practice are entirely separate fields
D. Social policy and social work practice are only slightly related

45. A 75 year old client meets with a social worker at a skilled nursing facility. Based on the client's report, the social worker suspects that the client is being physically abused by facility staff. The social worker should NEXT:

A. Conduct a comprehensive biopsychosocial-cultural-spiritual assessment
B. Report the suspected abuse to the local adult protective services agency
C. Consult a supervisor for further guidance

D. Report the suspected abuse to the facility director or his/her designee

46. Which of the following is NOT true regarding self-disclosure?

A. Self-disclosure is always unethical in social work practice
B. Some self-disclosure can be beneficial in therapy
C. Self-disclosure can at times be harmful to clients
D. Self-disclosure can potentially indicate a boundary violation

47. A client tells a social worker about cultural experiences in the client's life with which the social worker is not familiar. To best help this client, the social worker should use which of the following stances?

A. Cultural expertise
B. Cultural humility
C. Cultural brokering

48. When communicating with clients by email, social workers should NOT:

A. Send confidential client information in unencrypted messages
B. Take steps to protect the confidentiality of electronic communications
C. Develop policies and procedures for notifying clients of any breach of confidential information
D. Avoid sending messages for non-work-related purposes

49. Social workers accepting a barter as payment for services rendered is:

A. Always unethical
B. Ethical in rural communities only
C. Ethical in very limited circumstances

50. The difference between empathy and sympathy is that:

A. Empathy involves understanding or imagining how someone might feel, while sympathy involves sharing the feelings of another person

B. Sympathy involves understanding or imagining how someone might feel, while empathy involves sharing the feelings of another person

C. Empathy involves emotions that are explicitly stated while sympathy involves emotions that are not explicitly stated

D. Sympathy is relevant to social work practice while empathy is only used in non social work contexts

51. Which of the following is the primary reason for documentation in a client's chart in a hospital setting?

A. Continuity of care
B. Risk management
C. Legal requirements

52. At the hospital unit where you work, you notice that a colleague has been coming to work

late, failing to complete documentation, and frequently missing staff meetings. You are concerned about the impact of these behaviors on clients and on your team. What should you do FIRST?

    A. Report the colleague's behavior to your supervisor.
    B. Speak with the colleague about your concerns.
    C. Report the colleague's behavior to the state board.
    D. Ask other team members if they have noticed these behaviors.

53. A social worker at a community health center supervises a social work student intern. One day, when the intern returns from lunch, the social worker notices that the student smells of alcohol. Agency and school policies, as well as the state's social work regulations, do not allow the practice of social work while under the influence of alcohol. The student does not appear intoxicated, however, and is behaving normally. What should the social worker do NEXT?

A. Ignore the issue as the student is of legal drinking age

B. Speak with the student and have them go home for the rest of the day

C. Report the behavior to the agency security officer

D. Report the behavior to the student's school

54. All of the following are true about telemental health EXCEPT:

A. Telemental health services provide certain advantages, particularly with regard to access for clients living in areas with limited mental health services.

B. Telemental health services are exactly the same as in-person services and require no special considerations.

C. Social workers must obtain informed consent when providing telemental health services.

D. Social workers must consider the licensure requirements of the states in which they are licensed as well as the states in which clients are located.

55. At a Native American community health center, a White social worker is employed in an administrative role. While working in this role, the social worker should do all of the following EXCEPT:

A. Involve Native American people in service planning and provision
B. Seek out cultural competency training
C. Position the social worker as a cultural expert
D. Acknowledge the social worker's White privilege

56. All of the following are true about confidentiality EXCEPT:

A. In group settings, social workers should inform clients that confidentiality cannot be guaranteed.
B. Social workers must keep client information confidential, with no exceptions.

C. Social workers should discuss with clients their policies regarding confidentiality and its limits.

D. There are circumstances in which it is necessary to break confidentiality.

57. With regard to accepting payment for services, social workers should, in general, do all of the following EXCEPT:

A. Take into account the client's ability to pay

B. Accept payment in the form of goods or services

C. Explain their policies regarding payment and how non-payment will be handled

D. Accurately bill for services provided

58. In accordance with the Health Insurance Portability and Accountability Act, social workers have an obligation to:

A. Keep clients records confidential and obtain consent before releasing records

B. Warn and protect individuals who are being threatened by a client

C. Refer clients for psychological testing to obtain diagnostic clarification

D. Inform clients of which insurance plans the social worker accepts as a participating provider

59. A court-mandated client meets with a social worker for an initial session. The client tells the social worker that she will not be sharing any information, as she did not choose to be there. The social worker should NEXT:

A. Remind the client of the treatment goals

B. Acknowledge the client's lack of choice regarding treatment

C. Assure the client of absolute confidentiality

D. Explain the voluntary nature of social work services

60. A client reports having committed a violent crime against another adult for which he was not prosecuted. He then asks the social worker,

"You're not going to turn me in, are you?" The social worker should FIRST:

A. Report the crime to the authorities
B. Contact the victim to ascertain their wishes regarding prosecution
C. Reassure the client about confidentiality guidelines
D. Explore the client's feelings about the disclosure

Answer Key

1. **A**
2. **B**
3. **B**
4. **A**
5. **B**
6. **B**
7. **C**
8. **D**
9. **C**
10. **B**
11. **B**
12. **C**
13. **A**
14. **B**
15. **D**
16. **D**

17. **D**
18. **A**
19. **B**
20. **D**
21. **C**
22. **D**
23. **C**
24. **B**
25. **B**
26. **A**
27. **B**
28. **D**
29. **D**
30. **B**
31. **B**
32. **D**
33. **A**
34. **A**
35. **B**
36. **D**
37. **D**
38. **B**
39. **C**
40. **A**

41. **C**
42. **D**
43. **B**
44. **B**
45. **B**
46. **A**
47. **B**
48. **A**
49. **C**
50. **A**
51. **A**
52. **B**
53. **B**
54. **B**
55. **C**
56. **B**
57. **B**
58. **A**
59. **B**
60. **C**

Answer Explanations

1. **A.** Receipt of a subpoena from an attorney is not an ethical reason to disclose client information without consent. A subpoena is not the same as a court order, and an attorney who is not a judge does not have the authority to compel the release of records. In response to a subpoena, a social worker should file a motion to quash by claiming privilege and should not provide records unless a court order is issued. Even when in receipt of a court order, the social worker should attempt to limit the scope of records required, and should request that records remain under seal.

2. **B.** Social workers are considered mandated reporters and must contact their state's designated reporting agency any time that they suspect child

abuse or neglect. A report must be made regardless of a supervisor's assessment and even if the social worker does not have enough information to ascertain whether or not abuse has occurred.

3. **B.** This action is unethical, as the social worker should not prioritize their own self-interest over the interests of the client. According to the *NASW Code of Ethics*, social workers' primary responsibility is to promote client well-being. Clients' interests are, in general, the primary focus. The *Code of Ethics* further states that social workers are not to take unfair advantage of a professional relationship, nor should social workers exploit others for their own interests. In this example, the social worker's attempt to have the client include the social worker in his will would constitute taking unfair advantage as well as financial exploitation.

4. **A.** Social justice refers to the belief that every person deserves equal rights and opportunities. While one social justice related concept is equality, giving every person the same rights and resources, a challenge to this idea comes from the concept of

equity. Equity refers to the allocation of resources and opportunities based on the needs of individuals and groups, taking into account the privileges already in place in order to create equal outcomes. In social work, social justice is important at all levels, including micro, mezzo, and macro practice.

5. **B.** The social worker should decline the connection request. According to the *NASW Code of Ethics*, social workers should not accept requests from clients on social networking sites. This is to prevent boundary confusion, dual relationships, and potential harm. While this request is from a former client rather than from a current client, the same principles would apply as it is still important to prevent dual relationships with former clients.

6. **B.** Clients have a legal right to access their records, and the *NASW Code of Ethics* requires reasonable client access to records as well. The *Code of Ethics* further states that, when social workers have a concern that access to records could cause clients serious misunderstanding or harm, social workers should provide assistance in interpreting the

records. It is only in exceptional circumstances of potential for serious harm that social workers can withhold or limit clients' access to their records.

7. **C.** The social worker should refer the client to a colleague who has expertise in treating clients with psychotic disorders. According to the *NASW Code of Ethics*, social workers are required to refer clients to other professionals when those professionals' expertise is necessary based on the needs of the client. Further, the *Code of Ethics* states that social workers should provide services only within their areas of competence based on their education and professional experience. In this case, treating a client with schizophrenia requires substantial training and experience, which this social worker does not have, and therefore the best option is to refer to another professional.

8. **D.** The *NASW Code of Ethics* includes standards on cultural competence and diversity, which include the mandate that social workers demonstrate cultural awareness and cultural humility, engage in critical self-reflection, and obtain education

about diversity and oppression. Social workers can and do work with clients whose cultural backgrounds are different from their own.

9. **C.** One purpose of supervision in social work practice is to assist the social worker in addressing issues of countertransference. When countertransference issues arise, the social worker should discuss them in supervision in order to process the social worker's reactions while remaining available to meet the needs of the client and maintaining appropriate professional boundaries. While supervision does often have an administrative component, supervision should not focus primarily on administrative tasks. Supervision is necessary both for student interns and for social work professionals, and can be provided by licensed social workers as well as by other mental health professionals. For example, depending on state regulations, supervision hours may count toward clinical licensure when provided by licensed psychologists or board-certified psychiatrists.

10. **B.** According to the *NASW Code of Ethics*,

social workers are obligated to engage in social and political action in order to support the equal access of all people to the resources, services, and opportunities that they need. Further, the *Code of Ethics* states that social workers should support social and cultural diversity and act to prevent and eliminate exploitation and discrimination.

11. **B.** While dual relationships create the potential for many problems, and should often be avoided, they cannot and should not be avoided 100% of the time. Dual or multiple relationships occur when a social worker relates to clients in more than one role, which may be professional, social, and/or business. Dual relationships can create the potential for boundary crossing, and can pose ethical concerns. Because of this, dual or multiple relationships are at times unethical. According to the *NASW Code of Ethics*, social workers should not engage in dual or multiple relationships with current or former clients when they pose a risk of exploitation or harm. At the same time, dual or multiple relationships are at times unavoidable,

and must be navigated with clear, appropriate, and culturally sensitive boundaries.

12. **C.** Competence is listed as one of the core values in the *NASW Code of Ethics*. The *Code of Ethics* states, "Social workers practice within their areas of competence and develop and enhance their professional expertise."

13. **A.** The social worker should explore the clinical implications of attending or not attending the client's graduation ceremony. While the social worker has no obligation to attend, and can decline based on their own personal limits, attendance at a client's significant life event is generally permissible and ethical if handled with sensitive and appropriate boundaries. If a social worker does attend a client's life event, it should be at the request of the client. The social worker must be careful to maintain confidentiality of the social worker-client relationship.

14. **B.** The NASW Code of Ethics lists the following core values in its section on ethical

principles of the social work profession: service, social justice, dignity and worth of the person, importance of human relationships, integrity, and competence. Exploration is an important clinical technique, but it is not a core value.

15. **D.** Informed consent is the process by which a client grants a social worker and/or agency permission to use specific interventions. Informed consent should be based on a full disclosure of all information the client will need in order to make this decision. An informed consent document should include the purpose of the proposed treatment, risks of the proposed treatment, and any alternatives to the proposed treatment. This allows clients to decide for themselves whether or not they would like to proceed.

16. **D.** According to the *NASW Code of Ethics*, when social workers have direct knowledge of a colleague's impairment, they should first consult with that colleague when feasible and assist the colleague in taking remedial action. Only if the colleague has not taken adequate steps to address

the impairment should the social worker then take action through their employer, licensing board, or other organization.

17. **D.** Best practices for addressing burnout include practicing self-care, engaging in mindfulness activities, and connecting with other professionals. Further, a multi-faceted approach is often needed in cases of burnout, and so the correct answer is all of the above. Burnout takes the forms of depletion or exhaustion, increased distancing mentally from one's professional role, negativity or cynicism toward one's work, and reduced effectiveness in a professional role. Addressing burnout requires both structural and individual changes. At the individual level, addressing burnout requires multiple, ongoing forms of self-care (i.e., a lifestyle rather than a vacation), including mindfulness, along with engagement with a community of colleagues.

18. **A.** Consent can only be given by those who have reached the legal age of consent, which is typically 18 years old. Assent refers to an agreement

by an individual who is not able to give consent. Research with participants who are not capable of giving consent requires that the researcher obtain the consent of the parent or legal guardian as well as the assent of the research subject.

19. **B.** The concept of "duty to warn" (more accurately, "duty to warn and protect") refers to a mental health professional's obligation to inform potential victims, as well as the appropriate authorities, when a client threatens to physically harm others. In the United States, the concept of "duty to warn and protect" comes from case law, specifically *Tarasoff v. Regents of the University of California*. Similarly, in Canada, courts have found that the duty to warn others of imminent danger can outweigh professionals' responsibility to maintain client confidentiality.

20. **D.** According to the *NASW Code of Ethics*, social workers are expected to routinely review professional literature and participate in continuing education related to social work practice. This may consist of in-service training and/or outside

workshops. Clinical practice, such as conducting intake assessments and psychotherapy, does help social workers to strengthen their skills but is not considered a professional development activity.

21. **C.** Social work student interns should not identify themselves as social workers when providing services to clients, but rather should identify themselves as student interns. According to the *NASW Code of Ethics*, social workers should accurately represent their education and credentials to clients, agencies, and the public. Therefore, it is important for student interns to inform clients of this status. Student interns should inform clients of when their field practicum will end, in order to prepare clients for termination, and should also inform clients of their supervision arrangement so that clients are aware of what information will be shared and with whom.

22. **D.** Social workers are required to protect the confidentiality of client information. Social workers must protect written client records by keeping files in a secure location. When speaking

with colleagues about shared clients, social workers should avoid discussing confidential information in public or semipublic areas. In addition, when disclosing information to third parties, even with client consent, social workers should share only the minimum amount of information needed for the purpose of the disclosure.

23. **C.** Time management refers to activities intended to increase effectiveness and productivity. It is used in both business and personal applications. Time management techniques include categorizing activities based on importance and urgency. Addressing only urgent issues does not take into account the extent to which these issues may or may not be the most important ones to focus on.

24. **B.** Upon hiring a new employee, a social work administrator should review the job description with the employee and provide them with a copy of it. In a human resource management role, which this administrator is in, social workers should use a person-in-environment perspective in working with employees and should use best

practices to promote organizational effectiveness and equity. The use of job descriptions is one way to ensure that employees know what is expected of them, as well as to reduce bias in the hiring process.

25. **B.** Compassion fatigue includes both emotional and physical exhaustion that inhibit one's capacity to empathize and feel compassion for others. It is caused by exposure to traumatic material and may have a sudden, rapid onset. Its symptoms can mirror those of post traumatic stress disorder.

26. **A.** The social worker in an administrative and supervisory role should avoid, whenever possible, engaging in dual relationships with supervisees. According to the *NASW Code of Ethics*, social workers providing supervision or consultation should not engage in dual or multiple relationships that pose potential harm to the supervisee. In addition, social work supervisors must set clear, appropriate, and culturally sensitive boundaries. The *Code of Ethics* also states that social workers should provide supervision only within their areas of knowledge and competence.

27. **B.** As a part of cultural competence in working with LGBTQ clients, it is important that social workers acknowledge clients' pronouns and use the pronouns requested when referring to the client. According to published research, use of a chosen name and pronouns reduces depressive symptoms and suicidal ideation among transgender youth.

28. **D.** The social worker should first discuss these concerns with the colleague directly. According to the *NASW Code of Ethics*, social workers who become aware that a colleague is impaired due to substance abuse, mental health problems, or other personal problems should speak directly with that colleague when feasible in order to assist the colleague in addressing the issue. Only once this has been done, and if the colleague has not taken steps to address this impairment, should a social worker take action through other channels.

29. **D.** Occupational burnout is a common experience among social workers and includes symptoms such as physical exhaustion, increased

irritability, and feeling ineffective in one's work. Scheduling of vacations and taking personal time off represents one way in which social workers can combat the risk of burnout, but does not itself represent burnout.

30. **B.** When conducting couples therapy, it is especially important that social workers are attentive to issues of confidentiality. Social workers should seek agreement among the parties involved regarding confidentiality, and should share their policies regarding disclosure of information shared in couples counseling. In addition, social workers should discuss with clients how confidentiality will be handled if one partner shares information with the therapist outside of the couples' sessions.

31. **B.** It is very common for social workers to experience burnout, even if they practice self-care or have other resilience factors. Occupational burnout has many causes, including factors related to client work, organizational problems, and other contextual factors in the individual's life.

32. **D.** A social worker should not terminate services in order to pursue a business relationship with a client. According to the *NASW Code of Ethics*, section 1.17(d), "Social workers should not terminate services to pursue a social, financial, or sexual relationship with a client." Termination of services should take place when the goals of treatment have been met and when new goals have not been identified. Other reasons a social worker may initiate termination include referral to a provider who can better meet the client's needs, and in certain instances of non-payment. When terminating services due to non-payment, the social worker must inform the client of the balance due, discuss the consequences of non-payment with the client, and ensure that the client does not pose a danger to themself or others. If a client may need to change providers due to a change in insurance coverage, the social worker should discuss available options with the client and support the client in making an informed decision.

33. **A.** Social workers have an ethical obligation to protect client confidentiality. When served with

a subpoena, the social worker should object to it by filing a "Motion to Quash." A subpoena can be issued by a judge, a court clerk, or an attorney. While a subpoena cannot be ignored, it does not mean that the issuer has authority to compel the release of records unless it is accompanied by a court order signed by a judge.

34. **A.** The decision in *Tarasoff v. Regents of the University of California* established legal precedent for the principle that mental health professionals have a duty to warn individuals who are threatened with physical harm by a client. Duty to warn is thus one of the exceptions to social worker - client confidentiality.

35. **B.** Social workers' use of social media websites and applications creates the potential for boundary crossings. According to the *NASW Code of Ethics,* social workers should be aware of their personal affiliations and online presence and of how their involvement online may impact their ability to work effectively with particular clients. In addition, social workers should not accept

connection or friend requests from clients, and should not engage in personal relationships with clients on social media. However, social workers may use social media in professional ways without engaging in direct communication with clients.

36. **D.** Client information is to be kept confidential indefinitely, even after a client is deceased, with limited exceptions for cases in which the client poses a danger to themself or others, or in cases of suspected child abuse or elder abuse.

37. **D.** The best response is for the social worker to decline the former client's invitation. According to the *NASW Code of Ethics*, social workers should avoid engaging in dual or multiple relationships with clients when such dual or multiple relationships create the risk of exploitation or harm to the client. Further, social workers should not engage in sexual contact with current or former clients because of the potential harm that this would cause to the client. In this case, meeting for coffee or communicating through a mobile dating application would constitute a dual relationship and

could imply the potential for a sexual relationship. Ideally, the social worker would not respond at all through the app but would instead decline the request through more appropriate channels of communication. Even so, D is the best answer among the choices given.

38. **B.** An ethical dilemma refers to a situation in which a decision must be made in the face of two or more conflicting ethical values or principles. When faced with an ethical dilemma, a social worker must consider the multiple ethical issues at stake in order to determine the best course of action.

39. **C.** Professional codes of ethics, such as the *NASW Code of Ethics*, includes core values of the social work profession and ethical principles that social workers must follow. Codes of ethics do not provide a list of all possible ethical dilemmas, as there are always new situations that may occur in specific contexts. As such, it is not possible to provide step-by-step instructions for what to do in particular situations. In ethical dilemmas, social

workers must identify the ethical issues at stake in order to discern the appropriate course of action. Even so, codes of ethics do contain specific requirements, and ethical principles are, in this way, more than just recommendations.

40. **A.** The *NASW Code of Ethics* states that social workers should engage in social and political action to support equal access to resources and opportunities for all people, and to advocate for policies that improve social conditions. Social workers are required to take action to expand choice and opportunity for all people, with a focus on vulnerable and oppressed groups. While cultural competency training and processing countertransference are important, they do not adequately address the structural nature of racism.

41. **C.** While client self-determination is often a priority in social work practice, it is not always the main priority. This is because the social worker's obligation to the client must be balanced with the social worker's obligation to the larger society as well as certain legal obligations. In this way, there

are times in which the social worker's responsibilities to the larger society or to the law will supersede the social worker's responsibilities to the client. For example, a social worker is required to report if a client has abused or neglected a child, or is at risk of harming themself or others. The other statements listed are true: social workers are prohibited from having sex with current (and former) clients, and dual relationships should be avoided when possible.

42. **D.** In a therapeutic relationship, erotic transference is is a phenomenon in which a client shifts erotic feelings and desires from past attachments to the therapist. The social worker in this case must maintain appropriate boundaries while exploring the client's feelings.

43. **B.** The social worker's next action should be to seek cultural competency training and education relevant to Native American culture and specifically to the culture and customs of the tribe with which he is working. While asking clients about their cultural background and experiences

is sometimes appropriate, this is not an adequate next step in addressing the issue that this social worker is offending multiple clients and has found that he does not understand the cultural norms of the community in which he is working.

44. **B.** In many ways, social policy determines the ways in which social work is practiced. This is one reason that social workers should engage in social and political action, as policy decisions affect clients as well as social workers in many aspects of direct and indirect social work practice.

45. **B.** The social worker should report the suspected abuse to the local adult protective services agency. Social workers are legally mandated to report situations of elder abuse. Elder abuse reporting goes through state and local adult protective services (APS) agencies, which investigate and assess cases of suspected mistreatment of older adults as well as other vulnerable adults including abuse, neglect, and financial exploitation.

46. **A.** Self-disclosure, in general, is not an

unethical practice in social work. In fact, it can be beneficial to clients in some cases. However, self-disclosure can also at times can be harmful to clients, and can potentially indicate a boundary crossing or boundary violation. Self-disclosure should only be used when it will clearly be of benefit to the client, and social workers should seek supervision or consultation regarding the use of self-disclosure.

47. **B.** The social worker should use a stance of cultural humility. While cultural competence as a term implies a professional "knowing," cultural humility implies its opposite – not knowing. Instead of focusing on professional expertise or competence, cultural humility accepts that clients are far more knowledgeable about themselves and their experiences than practitioners can be. In this case, embracing a stance of cultural humility will lead the social worker to maintain self-awareness, a respectful attitude toward the client's cultural experience, and a valuing of the client's knowledge about their own experiences.

48. **A.** According to the *NASW Code of Ethics*, social workers should take reasonable steps to protect electronic communications, including safeguards such as encryption, firewalls, and passwords, in order to protect client confidentiality. Social workers should also develop policies and procedures for handling any breaches of confidential information, including notifying clients of any breach, and should avoid contacting clients through email for non-work-related purposes.

49. **C.** In very limited circumstances, it is acceptable for social workers to accept a barter of goods or services as payment for services rendered. However, the *NASW Code of Ethics* also states that bartering should be avoided in most cases. Social workers should explore and participate in bartering only when it is an accepted practice among professionals in the local community, when it is necessary in order for service provision, when it is negotiated without any coercion, and when it is initiated by the client and with the client's informed consent. The *Code of Ethics* further states that, when accepting goods or services as payment,

it is the responsibility of the social worker to be able to demonstrate that this arrangement will not be harmful to the client nor detrimental to the social work relationship. It is not a rule that only social workers in rural communities can engage in bartering.

50. **A.** The terms sympathy and empathy are often confused, even as distinctions between them are significant. Sympathy refers to one person sharing the feelings of another. For example, one may express their sympathy (their experience of sadness) when another person is grieving. Empathy, on the other hand, refers to the imagination or understanding of how another person may feel, even when the person showing empathy may not experience those same feelings. Empathic responding is an important aspect of a helping relationship.

51. **A.** The primary reason for documentation in a client's chart in a hospital setting is for continuity of care. Accurate, complete, and timely documentation allows for collaboration among the various professionals involved in a client's care.

This supports optimal decision making based on the most recent and complete information about a client's course of treatment, and prevents the duplication of services. While documentation does serve a risk management function and is necessary in order to meet legal requirements, these are not its primary purpose.

52. **B.** According to the *NASW Code of Ethics*, social workers who become aware of a colleague's impairment should consult directly with the colleague and assist them in remediating the impairment. Only if the colleague has not taken adequate steps to address the impairment, and if the impairment interferes with the colleague's practice, should a social worker take action through other channels such as the employer or licensing body.

53. **B.** The social worker should speak with the student about this behavior and have them go home for the remainder of the day. As a supervisor, the social worker is responsible for the student's ethical conduct and cannot allow them to remain in the clinic after drinking alcohol during work

hours. In this case, the social worker should discuss the issue directly with the supervisee in an effort to prevent this behavior from continuing. If it does continue, however, the social worker should then also take further action through appropriate channels.

54. **B.** Telemental health services provide certain advantages, especially in offering access to clients who live in areas with limited mental health services. To provide telemental health services, social workers must consider licensure requirements, especially if clients are located in different states. It is important to obtain informed consent from clients that specifically addresses the risks and benefits of this service. Telemental health services are not the same as in-person services and do require special consideration.

55. **C.** The social worker should involve Native American people in service planning and provision, seek out cultural competency training to learn best practices for working with Native American people, and acknowledge the social worker's White

privilege. However, the social worker should not position themself as a cultural expert – no matter how much they learn about the community in which they work. Rather, the social worker should adopt a stance of cultural humility and respect the knowledge and expertise of clients based on their lived experience.

56. **B.** While social workers must keep client information confidential, there are exceptions to confidentiality and circumstances in which it is necessary to break confidentiality. Social workers should discuss with clients their policies regarding confidentiality as well as limits to confidentiality. Additionally, in group settings, social workers should inform clients that they cannot guarantee that group members will keep information private.

57. **B.** With regard to accepting payment for services, social workers should take into account clients' ability to pay; should explain their policies regarding payment, including how non-payment will be handled; and should accurately bill for services provided. In general, social workers should

not accept payment in the form of goods or services. While bartering is not entirely prohibited by the *NASW Code of Ethics*, the *Code of Ethics* does state that social workers should avoid doing so, and that bartering may be acceptable only in very limited circumstances.

58. **A.** The Health Insurance Portability and Accountability Act, commonly known as HIPAA, requires healthcare providers to keep patient information confidential and to have safeguards in place to ensure the privacy and security of protected health information. Based on HIPAA regulations, social workers must keep protected health information secure and obtain consent for all disclosures that are not for the purposes of treatment, payment, or operations.

59. **B.** The social worker should next acknowledge the client's lack of choice regarding treatment. When working with court-mandated and other involuntary clients, social workers should pay attention to the challenges of engagement as well as their dual roles and responsibilities in relation to

the client and the court. The social worker's best response, and effort at building rapport in this instance, is to validate the client's experience. At this point there are not yet any treatment goals to refer back to. The social worker cannot assure any client of absolute confidentiality. In court mandated treatment there are particular limits to confidentiality as the social worker must report compliance or noncompliance, and possibly more detailed information, to the court. Further, the social worker should not describe services as voluntary, since this would not reflect the reality of the client's experience.

60. **C.** Disclosure of a past crime, regardless of the severity, is not an exception to confidentiality. While there are exceptions to confidentiality when a client is presently a danger to themself or others, this does not extend to past incidents of violence. The social worker should directly answer the client's question by clarifying policies regarding confidentiality.

Pass the LMSW Exam: A Practice Test for the ASWB Master's Level Social Work Licensing Examination
ISBN (paperback): 979-8986557007
ISBN (e-book): 979-8986557014

LMSW Passing Score: Your Comprehensive Guide to the ASWB Social Work Licensing Exam
ISBN (paperback): 979-8986557021
ISBN (hardcover): 979-8986557045
ISBN (e-book): 979-8986557038

LMSW Exam Prep Pocket Study Guide: Human Development and Behavior
ISBN (paperback): 979-8986557076
ISBN (e-book): 979-8986557083

ALSO BY JEREMY SCHWARTZ

LMSW Exam Prep Pocket Study Guide: Assessment and Intervention Planning
ISBN (paperback): 979-8986557052
ISBN (e-book): 979-8986557069

LMSW Exam Prep Pocket Study Guide: Intervention Methods and Theories
ISBN (paperback): 979-8986557090
ISBN (e-book): 978-1960339003